My First Pet Library from the **American Humane Association**

My First Bird

NEW HOPE

American Humane®

*Protecting
Children & Animals
Since 1877*

Enslow Elementary
an imprint of
Enslow Publishers, Inc.
40 Industrial Road
Box 398
Berkeley Heights, NJ 07922
USA

http://www.enslow.com

Linda Bozzo

American Humane®

Protecting
Children & Animals
Since 1877

Founded in 1877, the American Humane Association is the oldest national organization dedicated to protecting both children and animals. Through a network of child and animal protection agencies and individuals, the American Humane Association develops policies, legislation, curricula, and training programs to protect children and animals from abuse, neglect, and exploitation. To learn how you can support the vision of a nation where no child or animal will ever be a victim of willful abuse or neglect, visit www.americanhumane.org, phone (303) 792-9900, or write to the American Humane Association at 63 Inverness Drive East, Englewood, Colorado, 80112-5117.

● ●

This book is dedicated to my husband and daughters who never stop believing in me, and to pet lovers everywhere.

● ●

Library of Congress Cataloging-in-Publication Data

Bozzo, Linda.
    My first bird / Linda Bozzo.
        p. cm. — (My first pet library from the American Humane Association)
    Includes bibliographical references and index.
    ISBN-13: 978-0-7660-2749-7
    ISBN-10: 0-7660-2749-X
        1. Cage birds—Juvenile literature.
    I. American Humane Association. II. Title.
    III Series: Bozzo, Linda. My first pet library from the American Humane Association.
    SF461.35.B69 2007
    636.6—dc22   2006008405

Printed in the United States of America

10 9 8 7 6 5 4 3 2 1

To Our Readers: We have done our best to make sure all Internet Addresses in this book were active and appropriate when we went to press. However, the author and the publisher have no control over and assume no liability for the material available on those Internet sites or on other Web sites they may link to. Any comments or suggestions can be sent by e-mail to comments@enslow.com or to the address on the back cover.

Every effort has been made to locate all copyright holders of material used in this book. If any errors or omissions have occurred, corrections will be made in future editions of this book.

Illustration Credits: Arco Images/Alamy, p. 15 (top); courtesy of Larry DiMicco, pp. 21, 22; Eyewire, p. 14; image100, pp. 9 (top), 18, 27; Noel Hendrickson/Masterfile, p. 3; Photodisc, p. 10; Pixtal, p. 7; Shutterstock, pp. 1, 4, 5, 6, 8, 11, 12, 13, 15 (bottom), 16, 17, 19 (top and bottom), 20, 23, 24, 25, 26, 28, 29, 30.

Cover Credits: Shutterstock.

Contents

Wonderful Pets

Birds make wonderful pets. Just like you, they are smart. They like to play and are fun to watch. Bringing a new, **feathered** friend into your home can be exciting.

This book can help answer questions you may have about finding and caring for your new pet bird.

A Quaker Parrot

Parrots can make good pets.

What Kind of Bird Should I Get?

There are many kinds of birds to choose from. Some birds talk while others sing. Some birds are quiet. Birds come in many sizes. They come in many beautiful colors. Some birds can live a very long time. You will want to pick the perfect bird for you.

A purple-breasted red-headed Gouldian Finch

Birds come in many interesting colors.

These pretty birds are red, yellow, and green.

Where Should I Get a Pet Bird?

Ask a special bird **vet**, or animal doctor, where to get a bird. Other bird owners might also be glad to help. The bird you choose should be alert. Alert birds are lively and quick. This means they are healthy. An alert bird has been kept in a large, clean cage.

Make sure the bird you buy is alert.

A Lovebird

Ask a bird doctor to help you find the right pet bird.

What Will I Need to Buy for My Bird?

Your bird will want a cage it can call home. The cage you choose should have room for your bird. It needs room in its cage to flap its wings and fly.

perch

Birds like perches.

This African
Gray Parrot
likes its
toy ball.

Find a cage that is easy to clean. The cage should be safe and made just for pet birds.

Your bird will need a feeder and a water dish.

Do not forget, birds like to climb. They also like to jump. There should be at least two perches inside your bird's cage. Perches come in different shapes.

Toys can bring fun into your bird's cage. Some favorite bird toys are bells, swings, and mirrors. Birds also like toys they can peck and chew.

It is best to put a few different
toys in a bird's cage.

Where Should I Keep My New Pet?

Birds do not like to be alone. Your new pet will want to be near you. Place the cage in a safe place that is not too noisy. Be sure to keep your bird in a place where it will not get too warm or too cold. Keep your bird away from candles, smoke, and cleaning products. These can hurt your pet. Ask your vet if you are not sure about where to place your pet bird.

Keep an eye on your bird if you take it out of its cage.

Take time
to make
your bird's
cage a
fun place
to live.

Birds like
to play
together.

15

What Should I Feed My Bird?

Birds are like people. They like different foods. Some birds eat fruits and vegetables. Some eat seeds or **pellets**. Find which foods are best for your bird.

Give your bird fresh water to drink every day.

A Macaw

This bird enjoys seeds.

Western Rosella

How Should I Clean My Bird?

Birds like to keep clean. Some like to splash in a dish of water in the bottom of their cage. Some like a shower of warm water from a spray bottle.

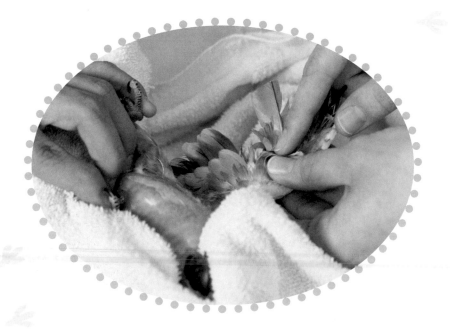

Your vet will make sure your bird is clean and healthy.

Keep your
bird clean
and it will
be happy.

How Often Should I Clean the Cage?

Birds can be messy. Change the paper in the bottom of the cage every day. Throw away old food and water. Wash the cage, once a week, with special soap made just for birds.

A Chinese White-eye

When you clean your bird's cage, check its droppings. Ask an adult for help.

Make sure you change your bird's food and water every day.

These birds enjoy
their perches.

Gouldian Finches

How Will I Know If My Bird Is Sick?

With good care most pet birds will stay healthy. But there are times when birds get sick.

Happy, healthy birds are both beautiful and fun.

24

Look closely at your birds each day to make sure they are healthy.

Watch for changes in your bird's droppings. A sick bird may hang its head. It may also have trouble perching. Check that your bird is eating and drinking. If you think your bird might be sick, see your vet.

A clean cage leads to a happy bird!

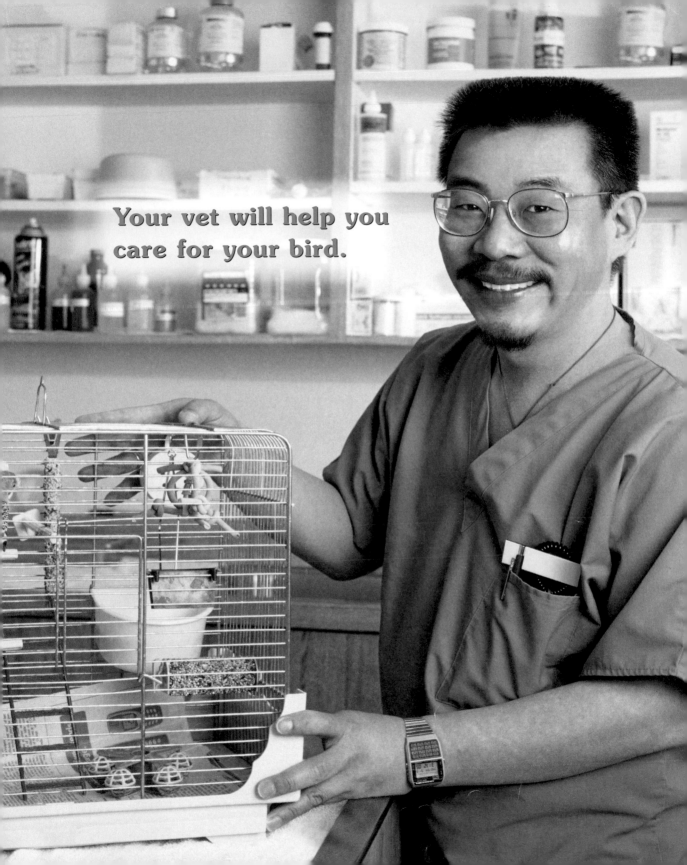

Your vet will help you
care for your bird.

You and Your Feathered Friend

Give your bird time to get used to its new home.
Be gentle. Love and care for your bird every day.
Your bird will be your feathered friend for many years.

Cockatiels

Parakeets

Words to Know

feathered—Having feathers. A bird is feathered.

pellets—A special type of food that is small and round in shape.

vet—Vet is short for veterinarian, a doctor who takes care of animals.

Read About

BOOKS

Blackaby, Susan. *A Bird For You; Caring for Your Bird.* Minneapolis, Minn.: Picture Window Books, 2003.

Frost, Helen. *Parrots.* Minneapolis, Minn.: Capstone Press, 2002.

Howard, Fran. *Parrots: Colorful Birds.* Minneapolis, Minn.: Capstone Press, 2005.

INTERNET ADDRESSES

American Humane Association
<http://www.americanhumane.org>
Learn more about animals at this Web site.

The American Society for the Prevention of Cruelty to Animals
<http://www.animaland.org>
Find out more about pet birds.

Index